SOUTHAMPTON CITY TRANSPORT BUSES

DAVID J. HUTCHINGS

AMBERLEY

This book is dedicated to my late parents John and Barbara Hutchings

First published 2021

Amberley Publishing
The Hill, Stroud
Gloucestershire, GL5 4EP

www.amberley-books.com

ISBN 978 1 4456 8169 6 (print)
ISBN 978 1 4456 8170 2 (ebook)

British Library Cataloguing in Publication Data.
A catalogue record for this book is available from the British Library.

Typesetting by Aura Technology and Software Services, India. Printed in the UK.

Introduction

This book of over 200 photographs attempts to illustrate the development of mainly diesel-powered buses operated by Southampton Corporation Transport and its successors since the early years of the twentieth century until recently.

It covers the vehicle types used, but also attempts to show as much background around the buses as possible to give a fuller portrait of this interesting city and its history.

Southampton Corporation purchased the horse tramway built by businessmen in 1879; the local authority electrified the tramways and in 1901 began running motor buses as an experiment. Bus services were used as feeders to the trams in the interwar years and a plan to convert to electric trolleybuses was put forward. The Second World War devastated the town and put paid to the trolleybus plan.

The last public tram service ran into Shirley Depot in the first hour of 1950. Diesel buses were to be the only public service in Southampton in the future. A large standardised fleet was built up until the last rear-entrance bus ran for the Transport Department in August 1981. Upon deregulation Citybus reintroduced rear-platform buses for a while, but the one-person-operated bus now holds sway.

New owners now run the buses; the story continues, but change never ends.

Author Bio

Born in Southampton, David J. Hutchings has had a lifelong interest in both local buses and railways. Now retired, he is a graduate of the University of Reading and trained as a horticulturist. He was glad of an opportunity to share the knowledge he has collected over the years from many friends and colleagues in the bus preservation world. He continues to live in Southampton.

Acknowledgements

Firstly, great thanks to those photographers who have allowed their work to be reproduced in this book – none of these images were produced by myself. In particular, members of the Solent Transport Trust (STT) and its later replacement the Southampton & District Transport Heritage Trust: the late Bill Windebank, David Norman and Ivan Bovey; and those still with us – Lister Newcombe, John Ashbridge, John Bulman, Thomas Lingwood, Adrian Willats, Jim Beckett, Keith Adams and Duncan Egerton. Also, outside the Trust: the late Fred York, Peter Relf, Peter Trevaskis, Phil Sposito, Eric Surfleet, R.H.G. Simpson, Robert Mack, Mike Cavendish, G. Cork, Norman Hamshere, S.L. Poole, Paul Hazlewood, P.C. Gurr and A.B. Cross. There are many others, and those whose work unfortunately remains unacknowledged.

If any image has been used without permission, I apologise and a correction will be made in any future editions. My warm thanks are also expressed to Steve Clitheroe and Thomas Lingwood, who have assisted me greatly with the computer work that I find difficult.

The author's royalties will all be donated to the S&DTHT to support its charitable work in restoring Southampton buses.

Fleet History of Southampton Corporation, City of Southampton Transport Department and Southampton City Transport Ltd (D.I. Gray, published by the PSV Circle) and *Southampton City Transport* (Ashley MacFarlane-Watt, published by Transport Publishing Company) was referred to when compiling this book.

Pre-war Buses and Trams in Southampton

AOW 265, SCT 62, new in 1937, is a Thornycroft Daring with Park Royal body H30/26R. Upon withdrawal in 1946 it went to work for Nottingham Corporation Transport as their no.125, and is seen here in NCT livery of green and cream. Note the lack of normal headlights and the installation of a radiator cover. Later it was used as a sports dressing room at Ruddington, Notts, a district that now hosts a transport museum. In July 1949, it was recorded at a farm near Loughborough. (Unknown)

CTR 310, SCT 75, a Leyland KP24 Cub with Park Royal B20F bodywork, is seen here in the middle of Southampton Common on Highfield Avenue. New in 1939, it appeared in 1948/9 in a green and cream livery lettered 'Jersey Airways' for operation to the airport. It is pictured here in standard livery. Serving SCT until 1955, it found a new home in Lincolnshire but was scrapped in March 1959. (S&DTHT Collection)

OW 7317, SCT 55, in Civic Centre Road on a service to Burgess Road via Hill Lane. The bus appears to be in the pre-war lined-out blue and ivory livery, which shows off its Park Royal B26F bodywork well. The bus was new in 1935, and with the clock tower being moved from New Road to Bitterne Park at about the same time the blinds would need to be updated. In the Second World War the Ministry of Supply took control for use as an ambulance and in 1948 it reached the scrapyard. (S.L. Poole/LBPG)

OW 7313, SCT 51, was new in 1935 and withdrawn in 1955 after completing twenty years of service, after which it was used by a contractor until being scrapped in 1958. It is seen here in Peartree Avenue on the eastern side of the River Itchen serving a route from the floating bridge. When new it was painted in the green and cream livery of Jersey Airways and used on the airport service from Central station until 1939. (S&DTHT Collection)

Above: CPC 17, SCT 48. New to Southampton in 1935, it was a a Leyland KP3 with Park Royal B26F body and demonstrator from Leyland Motors. Withdrawn in 1953, it was last recorded in a yard in Bugle Street the following year. It appears here after the war, off Archer's Road. It is thought to be laying over waiting for football fans coming from The Dell nearby. (Norman Hamshere)

Left: AOW 268, SCT 65. This Leyland Titan TD4 with Park Royal bodywork was put into fleet use in 1937; after a long life it was withdrawn in 1953 from SCT service. It served new owners in Kent until being scrapped in 1958. The advertisement for McDougall's Flour is very prominent. (Norman Hamshere)

CTR 508, SCT 28. This Leyland TD5 carrying Park Royal H30/26R bodywork was new in May 1939, withdrawn in 1951 and later used by West Sussex County Council. It is seen here at the floating bridge Southampton-side terminal in the post-war era. (Unknown)

BTR 68, SCT 39, a Leyland TD5 with Park Royal H30/26R bodywork. It is being used on a works service from the Thornycroft shipyard at Woolston, which can be seen in the background – note the new construction seen behind. This site is now covered by new development. New in 1938 and withdrawn in 1953, it went to Kent for further use. 39 was last licensed in December 1959. (S&DTHT Collection)

TR 9454, SCT 2. New in 1930 as one of a small batch of three with Park Royal H24/24R bodywork, it is seen here at New Road on route no.2. This bus was sold to Bournemouth Corporation in 1938, who got another twelve years of use from it.

OW 7238, SCT 18, is seen at Portswood Depot *c.* 1950. With H30/26R bodywork, it had a Gardner 5LW diesel engine that had five cylinders rather than the six later employed by SCT. New in 1935 and withdrawn in 1950, it was sold to the Hants Motor Company of Southampton and to North's in 1951. (W. Windebank/S&DTHT Collection)

BCR 224, SCT 67, was a Leyland TD5 with Park Royal H30/26R bodywork new in 1937. This image shows the bus in the pre-war lined-out blue and ivory livery. It was withdrawn in September 1955 and later scrapped in Surrey.

OW 4257, SCT 11, was a Thornycroft Daring DDAC/6 with AEC diesel engine. It was the first oil engine in the fleet. It had Park Royal H26/24R bodywork and was new in February 1934. Withdrawn by SCT in 1945, it worked for Skylark Motor Service of Salisbury until being withdrawn by them in July 1951. Note the prominent advert for the Grand Theatre, located next to the Hants & Dorset bus station in West Marlands. The theatre was demolished around 1959.

OW 5693, SCT 16, was a Guy Arab with 5LW Gardner engine. New in December 1934 with a Park Royal H30/26R body, it was withdrawn in 1949.

OW 7241, SCT 21, was a Guy Arab with 5LW Gardner engine new in December 1935 with a Park Royal H30/26R body. It was withdrawn in 1951 and sent to North's, a dealer near Leeds.

CTR 505, SCT 25, in Above Bar Street outside the Regal Cinema (later the Odeon) on its way to Bitterne Park Triangle in the pre-war livery. The Odeon was demolished over the winter of 1993/4.

CTR 503, SCT 23 – a Leyland TD5 with Park Royal H30/26R body new in 1939. It is seen here in Romsey Road, Shirley, in wartime livery with white-painted edges. It was withdrawn by SCT in 1951 and used by Valiant Coaches of London; by July 1955 it was with Chivers Contractors of Devizes, Wiltshire.

TR 22, ex-SCT 8, became tower wagon no. 102 in 1931 and is seen here before sale to Moon of Broadchalk, Wiltshire in 1950.

TR 9456, SCT 5. An AEC Regent with Park Royal H24/24R body new in November 1930, it is seen at work in Southampton on route 2. It was sold to Bournemouth Corporation in 1938 and eventually scrapped in 1950. It carries the pre-war blue and ivory livery.

TR 5185, SCT 30, a Guy B with SCT-built B26F body, new in May 1928 and withdrawn by 1939 before being sold.

TR 9453, SCT 45, a Thornycroft BC with Park Royal H24/24R body, new in 1930 and withdrawn in 1938. It was scrapped by the Corporation.

BTR 66, SCT 37. A Leyland TD5 with Park Royal H30/26R bodywork new in February 1938, it was withdrawn in 1953 and is seen outside the Thornycroft shipyard at Woolston.

BTR 874, SCT 5, was new in August 1938. It was a Leyland TD5 with Park Royal H30/26R bodywork. Seen at the New Road–Palmerston Road crossroads on service 1 from Woolston, it was withdrawn in 1953.

OW 7318, SCT 56, was Leyland Cub KPO3 with Park Royal B26F body. It is seen in Burgess Road near the recently demolished The Style pub. The tram tracks are still visible. New to SCT in September 1935, it was withdrawn in 1955.

OW 7320, SCT 58, a Leyland Cub KPO3 with Park Royal B26F. It was new in September 1935 and withdrawn in 1953 before being scrapped in St Denys by 1955. Seen at Woolston-side floating bridge bus terminal, probably on a summer's evening at 6.55 p.m. It is about to travel to Wright's Hill, not far away. Note the advert for the Great Show due to take place in Southampton, which may have taken place in the Bannister Park area.

CTR 507, SCT 27, a Leyland TD5 with Park Royal H30/26R body new in 1939 and withdrawn in 1951. Last known to be with Lefrey, London E14 in February 1958.

OW 7234, SCT 12. A Guy Arab 5LW Park Royal H30/26R new in September 1935, it was withdrawn in 1950 and sent for scrap in Leeds in 1951. It is seen at Portswood Depot with prominent side advert for Genasprin. (William Windebank/S&DTHT Collection)

OW 7238, SCT 18, a Guy Arab 5LW with Park Royal H30/26R body new in September 1935 and withdrawn in 1950 before being scrapped in Leeds in 1951. Seen at Portswood Depot probably in the scrap line, Belmont Road is visible in the background. (William Windebank/S&DTHT Collection)

OW 7312, SCT 50, a Leyland Cub KPO3 with B26F Park Royal bodywork. New in August 1935, it was withdrawn in 1953 and scrapped in St Denys by 1955. It is seen at the Woolston side of the floating bridge in about 1950 – note the Hants & Dorset bus to the right in its own bus station yard. When new it carried a green and cream livery and was lettered Jersey Airways. With the similar SCT 51, it operated a service to Eastleigh Airport until this was curtailed in September 1939. (A.B. Cross)

TR 271, ex-SCT 11, became tower wagon no. 101 in 1931 and was scrapped by the Corporation in around 1950.

Two former Leyland E 30hp buses, new in 1925 with SCT-built B25F bodies.

A 1930s view of Leyland Titans in St Denys Road garage of Portswood Depot. Note the proud staff and the truck delivering Esso diesel.

OW 7239, SCT 19. New in 1935 with a Park Royal body, this bus was withdrawn in 1950 and is seen here at Portswood Depot after a life of service to passengers. (S&DTHT Collection)

Southampton Corporation Tramways no. 91 is seen in Burgess Road near the junction with University Road in the post-war period. The tram is on route 1, on its way to Royal Pier via The Avenue. This car is one of standard height and would not have been able to go under the Bargate arch.

This photo, taken around 1959, is of tram no. 45 – the first tramcar to be preserved in the UK. It is seen here at the Montagu Motor Museum at Bealieu, Hampshire. In October 1960 it was moved by road via Southampton to Crich in Derbyshire, where it is looked after by the National Tramway Society.

Various buses in Terminus Terrace, sometime between May 1948 and December 1949. This can be deduced by the tram routes, which were withdrawn at these dates.

Fabulous 1950s

Guy Arab Single-deckers in Southampton

JOW 920, SCT 247, on a wet day at Pound Tree Road about to start on route 8 to Woolston. (R.H.G. Simpson)

JOW 920, SCT 247, turning into Pound Tree Road from Above Bar Street on route 8, captured *c.* 1960. The police phone post on the corner is now part of the past, like Jackson the tailor. (A.B. Cross)

JOW 917, SCT 244, turning from Above Bar Street into New Road, apparently on route 8. However, if the destination blind is correct it is going the wrong way. This image from the late 1950s shows Lloyds Bank in the background, which was later completely rebuilt, though this particular branch has now closed. (R.H.G. Simpson)

JOW 928, SCT 255, the last of the batch of twelve, is now preserved. The location in New Road has been totally transformed since this photo was taken in the late 1950s. The land is now under a major road gyratory system. (A.B. Cross)

JOW 918, SCT 245, still with rear-exit door, is in New Road. The buildings behind were swept away and now Solent University occupies the site. (Eric Surfleet)

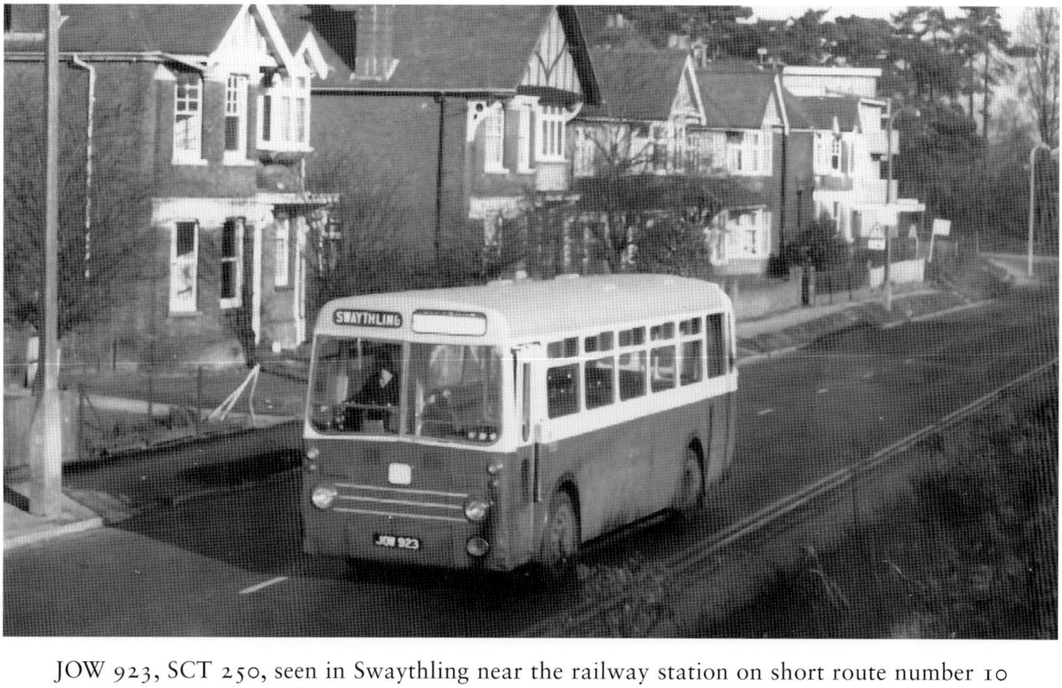

JOW 923, SCT 250, seen in Swaythling near the railway station on short route number 10 returning from South Stoneham Estate. The use of a single-decker is necessary due to the 'Black Arch' – Swaythling railway bridge. This view is now transformed by the removal of the houses and a dual carriageway leading to the M27 motorway.

STR 700, SCT 257. New in May 1957, it was an Albion MR9N Nimbus with Alexander B35F body. It was withdrawn by August 1972, but is seen here emerging from the infamous Swaythling Railway Arch on route 10 in June 1971. (Fred York)

Guy Arab Double-deckers in Southampton

DTR 460, SCT 33, is seen in Southampton Docks on an outing. This photograph was probably captured before 1964. This bus, with a 5-cylinder engine, was purchased in 1946 then converted to open-top in 1955. It was used on town tours from that year; later the department used it for tree-cutting and it was withdrawn in 1966. (Locomotion of Salisbury)

DTR 915, SCT 92, was a Guy Arab with Park Royal H30/26R body new in 1946 and powered by a Gardner 6LW diesel engine. Seen here opposite the Stile Inn in University Road – note the 'crest' type bus stop flag fixed to the post-war concrete bus shelter. The former Stile pub was demolished in summer 2019.

FTR 511, SCT 64. New in 1949 as a tram replacement bus, this image shows it on Sunday 2 May 1976 carrying the winning Saints football team after their success at Wembley in the FA Cup final the previous day. It is seen in Burgess Road running towards Swaythling – note the policeman sitting on the mudguard. A police Ford Transit minibus on security duty follows. This vehicle may have been manufactured at the factory nearby, which built these vans for many years. (Jim Beckett)

GTR 490, SCT 228, and GTR 470, SCT 208, in July 1969 in Portsmouth Road, Woolston. Both buses are either coming or going the short distance to the floating bridge bus terminus at the river's edge. The brick tower between is that of St Mary's Presbyterian Church, demolished in 1972. (Lister Newcombe)

GTR 485, SCT 223, on route 15 to Bassett Green, loading in Above Bar Street in July 1969. This is very close to where Southampton motor buses began to operate in 1919. BOW 501C, SCT 364, an AEC Regent V with Neepsend H37/29R new in 1965, is nearing the end of the very long route 4 as it passes on the opposite side of the street. (Lister Newcombe)

FTR 511, SCT 64, on a tour in the Western Docks following AEC Swift JOW 499E, which was new to Southampton in 1967. The AEC Swift has a Strachans body, which was built at Hamble just outside the city. (Unknown)

Seen on route 15 at Royal Pier in company with FOW 442 on route 9, no. 222 had an interesting life after SCT service ceased in July 1971. The bus is now in preservation in Hampshire after a lengthy restoration. (Lister Newcombe)

HTR 54, SCT 237, was new in 1952. This bus was fitted in 1958 with a heating and ventilating system devised by Cave-Brown-Cave, but modified by SCT. Withdrawn in 1970, it is seen here in Above Bar Street *c.* 1960. (Fred York)

LOW 218 was new in 1954 as part of the last batch of Guy Arab buses. It is one digit away from 71, the preserved example. Fitted with the SCT heating and ventilation system in 1956, it is seen here in 1965 at the terminus of route 15 – the Royal Pier. It was sold to Salisbury Group Hospitals in July 1972 for further use. (Unknown)

FOW 444, SCT 190, was new in 1950 and withdrawn in 1968, probably for scrap. It is seen here in the 1960s about to enter the High Street with The Sun, a temporary wood-framed prefabricated pub built on the remains of its bombed former building, visible to the left. The three ladies have probably just disembarked from the Hythe Ferry at its berth on Town Quay nearby. (P.M. Photography)

FTR 511, SCT 164, is seen here in Havelock Road *c.* 1970 about to depart on a docks tour. It was new in 1949 but converted to open-top in 1966 for this work. It became famous later under the fleet number 64 it still carries today. It is preserved and in the ownership of SCC Museums. (A.B. Cross)

GTR 476, SCT 214, was new in 1950 and withdrawn in June 1970. It is seen here in Pound Tree Road about to depart on route 1 to Woolston floating bridge via Bitterne and Itchen. It is a very wet day and the windows are well misted up with condensation. The advertisement for a well-known local wallpaper shop is very striking. (Mike Cavendish/Wessex Transport Society)

FCR 201 was a Guy Arab II new in 1948. After fourteen years of service it went to Gosport & Fareham Omnibus Company (Provincial) for use. It is seen here on their route 4 at Gosport Ferry terminus. It ended its life there in September 1971. (W. Windebank/S&DTHT)

FCR 203, SCT 113, was a Guy Arab III and is seen here at the floating bridge terminal (Southampton side). This bus was new in 1948 and had a Red Indian radiator cap, which were, and remain, much prized. The destination is set for the opposite floating bridge terminal at Woolston and will cross the river by way of Northam bridge. A Leyland follows. This bus later went to Scotland. The advertisement for the Gaiety Picture House is shielding a bomb site; this cinema operated in the high street from 1914 to 1956. (W. Windebank/S&DTHT)

FCR 443, SCT 142, was new in 1948 and can be seen in Burgess Road on route 11 destined for the docks. The fine advertisement for Bowyers Wonderful Wiltshire Sausages is prominent. In December 1964 it went to Provincial, but was not operated by them. The body was scrapped immediately and the chassis followed in 1968. (Unknown)

FCR 194, SCT 104, in New Road on route 6, is nearing the end of its long journey at Houndwell. Judging by the lady's dress this was taken in the 1950s. The bus, new in 1948 as a standard tram replacement, was withdrawn in 1962 before providing another four years of service with Graham's Bus Service in Paisley until probable scrapping. (Norman Hamshere)

FCR 449, SCT 148, is pictured in December 1964 in The Avenue. At this time the highway was two-way. Later, the parallel Inner Avenue was made southbound only and a one-way gyratory made of the two roads makes this view unrepeatable. (Unknown)

FCR 202, SCT 112, is at Royal Pier about to leave on the 15 to Bassett; the paper notice in the front window lets the public know it will serve Southampton Common – a practice undertaken to support Southampton Show, run by the council each July. This bus was new in 1948 and sold to Scottish operator AA Motor Services of Ayr, who never operated it. However, after donating its body to two buses its final withdrawal came in 1968. (Unknown)

SCT 81 in St Denys Road, opposite Portswood bus depot. Note the post-war bus stop flag. This photo was taken after trams were abandoned when the Bullar Road route was extended into the town centre, making a near loop. This was not to last.

SCT 32 in St Denys Road, taken after trams were abandoned when route 12 was extended to the town centre. The buildings behind still include a pub now called The Mitre, still a bus stopping location.

FTR 511, SCT 64, and FTR 514, SCT 67, in smart open-top condition in the Portswood Depot before its rebuilding. This photo was taken *c.* 1970.

FCR 444, SCT 143, was new July 1948 and withdrawn in 1964. It was converted to driver trainer in November 1965 as 902. It then became a play bus in Southampton. This photo is believed to show the bus after withdrawal by SCT, being converted at the Hants & Dorset body shop in Winchester Road. (Paul Hazlewood)

A standard SCT Guy Arab and a Hants & Dorset KSW with ECW highbridge body, at the downside of Southampton Central railway station yard. In the background the former Southampton Corporation coal-fired power station, built in 1903, can be seen. This provided electricity for the expanded tramway network but was demolished many years ago. Interesting cars are also shown, including a rare Standard Vanguard estate, a favourite with the RAF; a Rover P4; and a Ford Anglia with a Southampton registration. This photo was taken *c.* 1962.

SOUTHAMPTON
CORPORATION TRANSPORT
TIME & FARE TABLES

CORPORATION OMNIBUSES PROVIDE FREQUENT SERVICES TO SOUTHAMPTON'S SHOPPING CENTRE

1st Edition (A) — Commencing November, 1959
PRICE - THREEPENCE

G. ARMSTRONG, A.M.I.Mech.E., A.M.Inst.T.
General Manager and Engineer
226 PORTSWOOD ROAD
Telephone 54052/3

Advertising on the Southampton Corporation Omnibuses, Floating Bridges and in this timetable dealt with by the Publicity Department, Civic Centre, Southampton (Telephone 23855 Ext. 341)

Above: Shirley Depot, showing three Guy Arabs safe in their garage with two admiring bus enthusiasts or gricers taking notes – the very common form of youth transport in those days were push bikes, two of which are lent against the wall. This photo was taken *c.* 1960.

Left: SCT Fare & Time Tables November 1959 issue – price: 3*d*. The newly opened Edwin Jones department store can be seen at the left of the photograph. This large store became part of the Debenhams group and closed under that name in 2020.

Swinging 1960s

Leyland PD2 Double-deckers

303 TR, SCT 303, Leyland PD2/27 with Park Royal H37/29R bodywork new in March 1961. It has the 'Midland Red' style 'tin front' which did not give a clear view of the nearside footpath. This bus was withdrawn in January 1973, going to Essex but scrapped in the following November.

306 TR, SCT 306, is seen at the bus washing plant at Shirley Depot. New in 1961, it is a Leyland PD2/27 with the 'Midland Red' style front. Withdrawn in December 1972, it was converted into an open-top publicity vehicle for Eldridge, Pope brewers of Dorchester. It was last seen in South Wales but is believed now to be scrapped.

311 TR, SCT 310, Leyland PD2/27 with Park Royal H37/29R bodywork new in February 1961. Seen outside the offices of the Hants & Dorset Omnibus Station at West Marlands, it has the 'Midland Red' style front which had disadvantages, withdrawn in 1975. Behind is AEC Regent V BTR 361B SCT 361, which is preserved in Hampshire. (Phil Sposito)

324 AOW, SCT 324, Leyland PD2A/27, new in 1962 with Park Royal H37/29R bodywork, is seen here in the original cherry red with less cream relief on route 17 to Millbrook Estate in Pound Tree Road. Along with others of the same batch 324 was disposed of in 1977 to an unknown Southampton dealer. Similar 341 of 1963 is waiting to leave in the direction of Woolston carrying the later livery with more cream relief.

328 AOW, SCT 328, Leyland PD2A/27 with usual Park Royal H37/29R bodywork new in February 1962, withdrawn in September 1977 and scrapped by Booths of Rotherham in that year. It carried the more practical 'St Helens' type fibreglass radiator front, which improved appearance but more importantly gave better side vision for the driver.

336 AOW, SCT 336, Leyland PD2A/27 with Park Royal H37/29R body new in 1963 and withdrawn in 1978. It is photographed on the joint with Hants & Dorset route 54 to West End outside the Civic Centre. From the same batch 335 is safely preserved in Hampshire and runs very well. It has the St Helens-style glass fibre radiator front. (Unknown)

325 AOW, SCT 325, Leyland PD2A with Park Royal H37/29R bodywork new in February 1962 and worked for SCT until July 1977. It had an interesting life thereafter, going to Southampton Technical College as a vehicle to be used for apprentice training, and later for use with the Ambulance Service as a rescue vehicle by November 1984. However it has been scrapped since. S&DTHT have been successful in retaining parts for future incorporation in other preservation projects. It is seen here at Portswood Depot. (John Bulman)

302 TR, SCT 302, is seen at the Woolston side of the floating bridge. It is a Leyland PD2/27 with Tin front and Park Royal H37/29R body. New in March 1961 and withdrawn in 1972, it was scrapped by July 1980. Note the 'S' on the front of the bus indicating Shirley Depot, where it was based.

888 DUK, a Guy Arab V with Strachans H41/31F body new in 1963. It is seen here at Shirley Depot on loan to SCT during 1964 from Guy Motors Limited of Wolverhampton. (John Ashbridge)

AEC Regents

JCR 381E is on route 6 at the popular rose gardens in front of the Civic Centre – Southampton being the first city to coin that phrase for its municipal buildings. EEL 893C, a Hants & Dorset Bristol FLF, is loading for route 54 to West End, which was one of the few joint routes with SCT. The Hants & Dorset bus station offices can be seen to the right. Opened in 1934, they were designed in Portland stone to complement the impressive Civic Centre opposite. The 1960s office block replaced the brick Grand Theatre demolished in 1959. This block itself has now been totally transformed into residential accommodation. (Unknown)

KOW 909F, an AEC Regent V Neepsend H40/30R (SCB 401) new in November 1967. This photo was taken on 21 April 1991 on a tour to the Western Docks, which has seen a great deal of change since. The bus is now owned by a local bus dealer. (Unknown)

KOW 904F, SCT 396, seen at floating bridge terminal, Southampton, about to leave on service 17. New in November 1967 and withdrawn in 1981, it was still extant in November 1985.

KOW 905F, SCT 397, in a night-time view inside Shirley Depot, Carlisle Road, in December 1980. These buses were used a great deal on the busy route 17 between Millbrook Park and the floating bridge, when it still operated via Shirley. New in 1967 and withdrawn in 1981, it was reported to be in Germany. (P.C. Gurr)

KOW 905F, SCT 397, hard at work in Shirley Road on the 9A, probably after the Itchen Bridge was built. The building behind the Luton van was the former Shirley Library, which was based there from 1895 to 1969. (P.C. Gurr)

HCR 136D, SCT 379, a AEC Regent V with Neepsend H30/30R bodywork. Seen here at Portswood Depot. New in September 1966, it was withdrawn in 1980. (Unknown)

BOW 507C, SCT 100, an AEC Regent V with Neepsend H37/29R body, seen at a rally in Bristol in 1979. Alongside the bus is the late Dennis Forrest, a well-known local bus enthusiast and owner. The bus is in pre-war blue and ivory Southampton Corporation Motor Service livery, which was especially applied for the 100th anniversary of Southampton transport in 1979. It is now preserved in Hampshire. (S&DTHT Collection)

Another view of the same bus (BOW 507C) at a Southsea Rally *c.* 1979. Formerly SCT 347, it was an AEC Regent V with East Lancs H37/29R body new to SCT in 1963. (Unknown)

BOW 503C, SCT 366, seen in Above Bar Street by the *Titanic* engineer's memorial. It is on route 11, giving service between northern Southampton and the Eastern Docks. Hants & Dorset UEL 724, a Bristol/ECW H33/27R new in 1958, is in hot pursuit but not in competition. (Robert Mack)

BOW 503C, SCT 366, seen at Vincent's Walk. New in January 1965, it was withdrawn in 1979 and after passing through many owners it is now preserved.

318 AOW, SCT 318, is seen when new in 1962 in original cherry red livery with limited light cream relief. An inside paper slip advert for C&A Modes Sales is in the window, but the larger outside adverts have not yet been applied. It is seen at the floating bridge terminal in Woolston. This bus is preserved in Hampshire. (Lister Newcombe)

Above: 367 FCR, SCT 347. New in 1963, it was a standard AEC Regent withdrawn in 1978 and converted into a playbus by the Southampton & District Playbus Scheme before later going to Wildern School of Motoring. It is seen here behind a band on Castle Way in the Southampton carnival on 18 July 1981. (Unknown)

Left: JCR 383E, SCT 394, an AEC Regent V with Neepsend body H40/30R, new in September 1967 and withdrawn in 1981. It is seen here in Oakbank Road, Woolston, during rerouting before the construction of the Itchen Bridge, which opened in June 1977.

Another of the long AEC Regent double-deck buses on route 11 turns from Bernard Street into High Street at Holy Rood. The public house behind the bus was named The Nag's Head. (Unknown)

One of the long AEC Regent double-deck buses on route 17A, turning from Commercial Road into Above Bar Street at Town Junction. The two former tramway transmission poles utilised for city council publicity can be seen advertising Southampton Show in the summer of 1972. The building behind the bus now demolished was, for many years, the city information bureau. Four K6 telephone kiosks are aligned alongside under the sign. All this has been swept away. (Unknown)

AEC Regent V from the 1962 batch, with the as delivered dark cherry red livery with minimal cream relief. It is seen at the floating bridge terminus at Southampton when new, alongside a Guy Arab III and a new Leyland PD2A. All have Park Royal bodywork. The Regent is about to depart for Peach Road on the frequent route 9A. (S&DTHT Collection)

314 AOW, SCT 314. An AEC Regent with Park Royal H37/29R bodywork new in February 1962, it is seen outside Shirley Depot in Carlisle Road. This bus was withdrawn in 1975, but by 1976 went to France where it remains. To the left of the image is a former tramways transmission pole utilised for extra lighting of the depot forecourt. It is painted light grey with a royal blue base. (John Ashbridge)

366 FCR, SCT 346. An AEC Regent V with East Lancs H37/29R body new in November 1963, it was withdrawn by SCT in November 1975 and cannibalised for spares by the Corporation. The remains went for scrap in July 1978. It features in a rear view of several buses in Pound Tree Road during the 1960s. (S&DTHT Collection)

368 FCR, SCT 348, was an AEC Regent V with East Lancs H37/29R bodywork. New in November 1963, it was withdrawn for cannibalisation in November 1978. It is being followed through the bus wash at Portswood Depot by BCR 377K, SCT 13 – a Seddon Pennine RU with Seddon B44F single-deck body. No. 13 was new in February 1972 and cannibalised from January 1981. This magnificent image shows the buses in a wet shiny light.

377 FCR, SCT 357, was an AEC Regent V with East Lancs H37/29R bodywork new in November 1963 and seen here in Pound Tree Road bus centre in June 1965. Note the bus driver wearing his summer jacket. It is about to commence route 8 to Woolston via Kathleen Road and Weston. This bus had an interesting life after withdrawal in 1979, going for non-PSV driver training duties with British Airways near London. It was exported to Eindhoven, Holland, in May 1981. (Peter Trevaskis)

376 FCR, SCT 356. An AEC Regent V with East Lancs H37/29R bodywork new in November 1963 and withdrawn in 1979, it is seen here in the withdrawal line at Portswood Depot. 356 was retained by SCT for engineering apprentices training but the remains were scrapped locally in January 1980.

365 FCR, SCT 345, an AEC Regent V with East Lancs H37/29R body, new in November 1963 and withdrawn in 1978. Cannibalised for spares by SCT, it was scrapped locally by April 1980. It is seen here at New Road about to turn into Above Bar Street alongside a Post Office Austin/Morris J2 van DTR 50K, which is now very rare itself.

JCR 384E, SCT 384, an AEC Regent V with East Lancs H40/30R body new in January 1967 and withdrawn in 1978. It was used in the Superbus competition in Liverpool in October 1980. No. 384 is overtaking 342 AOW, SCT 342, a Leyland PD2A/27 with Park Royal body. They are in Above Bar Street, both on their way to be nearer to the water. Note the radiator cap flap on no. 342 is missing.

HCR 136D, SCT 379. This AEC Regent V with Neepsend H40/30R body on East Lancs frames was new in September 1966 and withdrawn to Rotherham by June. Seen alongside 316 AOW, SCT 316, an AEC Regent V with Park Royal body, is seen at the Southampton side of the floating bridge bus terminal.

TCR 293–6H, SCT 7–10, AEC Swifts with East Lancs B47D single-deck buses new in 1969. They were withdrawn in 1980 and went to Booth's, a dealer. They are seen here at Portswood Depot in 1978. (John Ashbridge)

Shirley Depot yard, with Leyland Titans and Guy Arab buses alongside contemporary cars – two old black Fords and a colourful two-tone Vauxhall Cresta.

A joint Southampton City and Hants & Dorset bus stop flag.

A maker's plate from Strachans bodybuilders, based in Hamble, Hampshire.

Diesel-powered floating bridge taken before 1972 and the construction of the Itchen Bridge. The bridge is mid-river. Note the SCT buses to the right of the image on the Woolston side.

The floating bridge terminal on the Woolston side. The church tower was demolished in 1972, therefore this image must precede this date. Hants & Dorset buses are in their own bus station, which closed *c.* 1970.

The floating bridge across the River Itchen was operated by SCT since the 1930s. This 1960s diesel bridge is loading on the Southampton side before June 1977, when the service ceased. The person at the controls was called a driver and it is powered by the same type of engine fitted to Leyland Atlantean buses. Note the fine warships being fitted out at Vosper Thornycroft shipyard on the Woolston side.

The diesel floating bridge at the Southampton side, with the new Itchen Bridge in the background. This replaced the 'floaters' in June 1977.

Taken on Wednesday 31 July 2019, on the occasion of the 100th anniversary of Southampton Transport, here preserved AEC Regent BTR 367B crosses Itchen Bridge. This was opened for traffic in June 1977 and named by H.R.H. Princess Alexandra later that summer. This bridge completely transformed bus services in Southampton for the better. (Chris Drew)

Leyland Atlanteans

UPO 234T, SCB 234, at Lordshill in the all-over red livery, about to depart for Sholing. Sister 229 has a small replacement panel in the old cream colour, probably fitted from another vehicle. 1 May 1992.

FTR 267X, SCB 267, at Vincent's Walk on route 6. The building behind was used for retail purposes after the war, but was a Hendy Ford showroom until 1940 when it was taken over for Spitfire production under the dispersal scheme. Now demolished, the site has hosted student accommodation since 2017. 10 August 1990.

HTR 559P, SCB 189, carrying the all-over red livery with black relief seen in Pound Tree Road, which was adapted as the bus centre in May 1959. The bus was new in November 1975. 10 October 1990.

UPO 245T, SCB 245, at Southampton Central railway station on the Hydrobus route 91, linking with the Red Funnel ferries to the Isle of Wight. 1 October 1989.

YRV 250V, SCB 250, in the all-over red livery. For decades Southampton brush-painted vehicles at Portswood Depot; this was the last one completed. This photo is a small tribute to the painter's decades of work. 1 May 1992.

PBP 222S, SCB 222. This image is recorded as a contrast to its former fleet mate, Guy Arab GTR 484 (SCT 222), now magnificently restored and preserved in Hampshire. 13 May 1992.

KOW 276Y, SCB 276, in all-over red livery at Lordshill. In the background the similar HTR 557P, SCB 195, can be seen. After service this bus was used by Black & White, based in Winchester and Andover. It saw out its life as a stores bus and spares donor in preservation for S&DTHT until scrapped in 2018. Numerically 276 was the last Leyland Atlantean delivered to Southampton City Transport Department; from the same batch fleet number 274 is preserved in Hampshire. 15 May 1992.

KOW 274Y, SCB 274, in Vincent's Walk – known as 'back of the stores' – in Southampton city centre on route 27 to Lordshill. New in November 1982, it was placed in an all-over 'Save Our Buses' livery in 1984. In relation to bus deregulation in 1986, this bus visited Strasbourg in October of that same year. It is preserved in Hampshire. In the foreground a 'Southampton' type seat can be seen. For many years, these were produced by Neptune Concrete Products at Bitterne Manor. 16 October 1986.

EOW 401L, SCB 168, seen at Lordshill in all-over red livery. It was new in 1972. EOW 400L, from the same batch, is in preservation and left for new Lancashire owners in 2019. All original Southampton Leyland Atlanteans carried East Lancs bodywork. 15 August 1992.

EOW 402L, SCT 169, is seen at Lordshill. It was from the same batch as 168 and is in the red and cream livery dating from before bus deregulation. The Ford Cortina is also a blast from the past in both colour and model. 19 June 1986.

XTP 277L, SCB 509, is seen at a Netley Bus Rally on service as an information point for the bus company. The two pairs of doors are a help in this role. It is a Leyland Atlantean AN68/1R with Alexander body H45/30D, new in June 1973 to City of Portsmouth Passenger Transport Department. When the two organisations were joined for a period, this bus came to Portswood. It is seen in the then current all-over red livery. 15 July 1990.

WOW 529J, SCB 507. Originally new in 1971 as SCT 139, it was converted to open-top in March 1984 for use on tours and later heritage use. It is seen on hire for a Scouts event near Sainsbury's supermarket in Lordshill. It is now in preservation, but since 2018 has carried registration WOW 531J. This was obtained from sister bus SCT 141, which was scrapped the same year. 21 April 1990.

WOW 529J, again as SCT 900, in traditional livery on its East Lancs O45/31F bodywork. It is on City Tour duty outside the Geddes Warehouse built in 1866, which has been used as apartments for many years. 22 April 1984.

WOW 529J in newly applied Red Ensign livery, seen in Shirley High Street. Note the red wheels instead of black. It has passengers and is about to depart. This bus is preserved in Dorset and now carries index mark WOW 531J. 19 June 1988.

ERV 249D, new to City of Portsmouth Passenger Transport Department in 1966. It is a Leyland Atlantean PDR 1/1 mark II carrying MCCW O43/33F open-top bodywork. It is seen at a Netley Bus Rally *c.* 1990 carrying Red Ensign livery as number 506. It was withdrawn in 1991. Similar ERV 251D, former CPPTD 11, from the same batch is preserved in Hampshire.

TTR 163H, former SCT 129, seen in the livery of Taff Ely Transport at their Glyntaff depot. Taff Ely owned and operated this bus in their azure blue/white colours as 82 from May 1983 until October 1986. It never operated for Taff Ely after bus deregulation that month and was disposed of. 11 July 1984. (Unknown)

TTR 167H, former SCT 133, was new in 1970 and converted to take wheelchairs for the 'Wheels on Wheels' service as H45/17F (with space for four wheelchairs) in June 1985. Later, wheelchair accommodation was increased. A special livery was applied at Portswood Depot, where this image was recorded. It is now preserved in Hampshire in its original livery.

TTR 156H, SCT 122, was a Leyland Atlantean PDR1A/1 with East Lancs body H45/31F. New in 1969, it was converted to a driver training role as 920 from August 1981 and withdrawn in June 1991. It is seen at Pound Tree Road. Note the small extra window on the off-side.

STK 126T, new to Plymouth Citybus in April 1979, was a Leyland Atlantean AN68A/1R with H43/28D Roe bodywork. It was purchased by Southampton in 1992 and the second passenger door was removed. It is seen here in all-over red livery in Above Bar Street. Similar STK 125T is still in existence as an open-top bus, and was also used by Southampton.

PCR 308M, SCT 185, was a Leyland Atlantean AN68/1R with East Lancs H45/31F bodywork new in June 1974. Upon withdrawal in October 1991 it went to Bristol as a playbus. KOW 905F, an AEC Regent V with Neepsend H40/30R bodywork new in September 1967, went to West Germany upon withdrawal in October 1981. This photo was taken at Vincent's Walk in the buses area. An advertisement for *The Sound of Music* is prominent; it was to be performed at the then Gaumont Theatre, which is now the fully commercial Mayflower Theatre. (*Southern Echo*)

OJI 1871, reregistered from HTR 567P. A Leyland Atlantean AN68/1R, it was new in November 1975 as a standard double-deck Leyland Atlantean SCT 198. It was rebuilt into single-deck form as an experiment in 1991, making the B35F 'Sprint' class and being reregistered as OJI 1871 (SCB 351) in 1991. This was not particularly successful. It was eventually withdrawn from service in Southampton. 15 May 1992.

WOW 530J, SCT 140, is seen in Mallard Road Bus Depot, Bournemouth, at an open day. This bus was being used by The Spirit of Endeavour. It was in service with SCT from July 1971 until September 1986.

WOW 527J, SCT 137, is seen at Portswood Depot in use as a hospitality bus. It was new to SCT in February 1971 and withdrawn in July 1986. This bus survived until October 2014.

Three Leyland Atlanteans at the bus terminal of the floating bridge, on the Southampton side. This large area was constructed in the post-war years after the end of the tram service. This facility was closed upon the opening of the Itchen Bridge in 1977.

TTR 167H, ex-SCT 133, in its 'Wheels on Wheels' guise in Vincent's Walk with two Routemasters.

Rear ends of standard Southampton Leyland Atlanteans in smart red and cream livery, showing their bustles at Portswood Depot.

Portswood Depot, Belmont Road side, with three standard SCT Leyland Atlantean/East Lancs in the picture.

After Deregulation

WLT 564, ex-LT RM 564. SCB 406 was an AEC with Leyland engine and Park Royal H36/28R body. New in December 1960 to London Transport, it is seen here during the bus war of the 1980s, turning into Hanover Buildings on its way to Weston followed by a competitor. The earlier large fleet name is clearly visible. It was sold to Japan for use as a wine bar in October 1989.

ALD 969B, ex-LT RM 1969. SCB 417 was an AEC with Leyland engine, and is seen outside the much-missed Plummers department store in Above Bar Street. It was new to London Transport in July 1964 and bought by SCB in 1988, then exported to the USA in 1990.

ALM 5B, ex-LT RM 2005. SCB 407 had been new to London Transport in September 1964, again with a Leyland engine, and later withdrawn. It was used by Southend Transport in February 1989 as their number 114. It is seen here turning from Hanover Buildings into Vincent's Walk, en route to Millbrook Estate. It was exported to Rathcole, Ireland, in March 1994 and destroyed by arson in April 2011.

363 CLT, ex-LT RM 1363, seen at Lordshill as SCB 405. New to London Transport in December 1962, it came to Southampton in May 1987 and was withdrawn exactly a year later. It left Portswood Depot the following December to an unknown fate.

654 DYE, ex-LT RM 1654. SCB 418 was new to London Transport in July 1963 and came to Southampton in January 1988, taking on Citybus red livery. It is seen in Lordshill with the smaller fleet name, as if on service to Weston. Upon withdrawal in October 1990 it passed to Dennis Forrest for preservation.

654 DYE. The same bus is seen at Southampton Central railway station. This may well be an image captured after preservation.

ALM 37B, an ex-London Transport Routemaster at work in Southampton as SCB 404. Here it is turning into Pound Tree Road during the 1980s.

A277 ROW, SCT 277, on the corner of Above Bar Street, turning into Pound Tree Road on route 24 in the usual standard Southampton livery before deregulation, which occurred in October 1986. This bus was new in April 1984. It was powered by a Gardner engine running through a Maxwell gearbox.

A277 ROW, SCT 277, with a East Lancs H46/30F body. It is seen at Shirley Precinct on route 9 from Weston to Lordshill in reversed Southampton City Transport livery on 27 June 1986.

A280 ROW, SCT 280, at the top of London Road adorned with City of Southampton crests. It carried reverse standard livery and transferred, along with many others, to Southampton City Transport Ltd on 26 October 1986.

E290 HRV, SCB 290, seen with Southampton Citybus/Red Ensign livery and Gardner engine. Similar 289 is preserved in Hampshire. 21 May 1991.

G302 SCR, SCB 302, a Dennis Dart/Duple B36F, seen in Pound Tree Road. It was new in February 1990.

GTP 95X, SCB 300. This Dennis Lancet/Wadham Stringer DP 33F was new in February 1982 to Portsmouth Corporation. It had a period of loan to Brighton Borough Transport in 1991 to 1992, and was also with Thamesdown. Acquired by SCB in October 1989, it has since been scrapped.

N329 ECR, a Dennis Dart in red First livery, is seen standing alongside the site of Hendy's Ford car showroom in Vincent's Walk. This location was used for Spitfire production during the Second World War.

ERV 117W, Portsmouth City Bus 117, was a Leyland National 2 with B41F body new in July 1981 to CPPTD of Portsmouth. It was on loan to Southampton from 1 September 1988 to 12 December 1988 and is seen here on service in Vincent's Walk. (Lister Newcombe)

F103 RTR, SCB 103, was a Leyland Lynx and can be seen on Citybus route 52 service between Southampton and Petersfield. This photo was taken outside the now closed Moorgreen Hospital, which had the use of a very large and well-built bus shelter that has sadly now been removed.

G105 WRV, SCB 105, in red Citybus livery at Lordshill. It was new in 1990.

G111 XOW, SCB 111, at Lordshill. This bus is now in private ownership and awaiting restoration.

TRN 461V, an ex-Cumberland Motor Services Bristol VR with ECW bodywork seen in the livery of Solent Blueline in the 1980s at Ocean Village. This view is included to show the Calshot lightship built in 1914 at the Thornycroft yard at Woolston on the opposite bank of the River Itchen. Behind the vessel is the former railway-owned continental booking office, through which Burgess and Maclean escaped to France by BR ferry in May 1951. This building has unfortunately been demolished, but the lightship is preserved. (Lister Newcombe)

D54 ERV, SCB 54. This Fiat/Iveco with Robin Hood B21F body was new in January 1987 and is seen here in Citylynx livery at Lordshill in May 1989. It left in December 1990 for further service with Southern National of Taunton.

D54 ERV, SCB 54, is seen in the original Southampton Citybus livery in April 1987, when only a few months old.

E55 LBK, SCB 49, a MCW with B25F body, is seen in Citylynx livery at a Portswood Depot open day on 9 July 1988 alongside eager local bus photographers. Behind is a SCC mobile library mounted on a Ford passenger coach chassis. In February 1990 the MCW was sold to Strathclyde Buses in Glasgow.

A Southampton City bus welcome sign.

A post-war bus stop flag, as employed throughout Southampton by SCT for several decades.

Preservation

Above: LOW 217, SCT 71, with Park Royal H30/26R bodywork. New in 1954, it is now in preservation and has been owned by Southampton City Museums since 1986. It is seen here in central London on duty for enthusiasts. This bus sports an excellent repaint, but the destination blind is highly misleading. (Lister Newcombe)

Right: FTR 511, SCT 64, in preservation at Riverside Park, Southampton, after a community event in 2014. (Tom Lingwood)

SCTs 64 (FTR 511), 222 (GTR 484) and 71 (LOW 217) in Above Bar Street on 11 June 2018 during the re-entry of 222 into Southampton following extensive restoration work. (John Ashbridge)

LOW 217, SCT 71, in preservation. It is dressed to appear as a wartime bus for the fiftieth anniversary of D-Day in 1994, at the National Motor Museum, Beaulieu.

FTR 511, SCT 64, in resplendent newly painted livery, complete with centenary advert panel, in the rebuilt Portswood Depot. The Leyland Atlantean to the rear, WOW 540J, SCT 150, was new in April 1971 and had an interesting life after withdrawal in September 1986, being converted into a mobile cinema. It was reacquired by Southampton Citybus in December 1989 as their 508. It is not known when this image was recorded.

JOW 928, SCT 255, a Guy UF with Park Royal body, resplendent and newly repainted by its owners the Solent Transport Trust (STT) after an earlier restoration. It is seen at the STT base in Bishop's Waltham. (S&DTHT Colllection)

JOW 928, SCT 255. A Guy UF with Park Royal Standee-type body, it was new in 1955 (chassis, 1952). It was purchased for preservation in 1976. It is viewed here being towed from a farm in Blendworth, Hampshire, to Hook by Warsash for further restoration in 1979. (John Ashbridge)

370 FCR, ex-SCT 350, with BCR 379K and other preserved buses at a Netley rally. This AEC Regent V with East Lancs H37/29R bodywork was new in November 1963 and also saw use as a training bus until withdrawal in 1981. Since then it has been in preservation and in use in France as a classroom. It is now in preservation again in Hampshire. (Adrian Willats)

JOW 499E, SCT 1, in preservation service in September 2016 at Bugle Street, Southampton.

BTR 361B, an AEC Regent V with East Lancs H37/29R bodywork that was new in June 1964. In preservation from July 1979 with members of the Solent Transport Trust. Members can be seen here working on the bus at the then-current STT base in Bishop's Waltham, *c.* 1990.

BCR 377K, SCT 15, a Seddon Pennine RU with Seddon B44F single-deck body. It was new in March 1972 and is seen here at the Netley Bus Rally in 1984. Subsequently preserved by members of the Solent Transport Trust, it is now owned by S&DTHT itself and awaits restoration. (Adrian Willats)

JOW 499E, SCT 1, an AEC Swift in preservation, offering a free bus link from outside Dock Gate 4, Southampton. A Leyland Panther from Winchester is assisting along with 318 AOW, SCT 318, and FTR 511, SCT 64. The red-brick building in the background was the docks post office and telegraphs office, but now contains apartments. The road layout has since been changed completely.

FTR 511, SCT 64, BTR 361B, SCT 361, and BOW 507C, SCT 371, in a line-up. 371 was repainted into pre-war SCT blue and ivory livery, fully lined out, and renumbered 100 for the Southampton Transport 100th anniversary in 1979.

A display of preserved buses in Southampton Eastern Docks at a fifteenth anniversary event for S&DTHT. From left to right: JOW 499E, SCT 1; KOW 274Y; TTR 167H; ALM 37B, SCB 404; KOW 910F, SCT 402; LOW 217, SCT 71. (Tom Lingwood)

TTR 167H, ex-SCT133, is seen in the Eastern Docks at berth 48 serving the steamship *Shieldhall* while in preservation. (Angela Smith)

The Southampton & District Transport Heritage Trust roundel. This echoes the former design of SCT tram and bus stop flags utilizing the Southampton crest. The charity has always put effort into good design, presentation and the use of a single font in its output.